Drawing Straight Lines

To parents
This exercise is to practice drawing lines with a pencil. Being able to draw steady lines without much difficulty, will allow your child to write numbers properly. You may give your child some hints like, "Let's draw a line from the balloon to the other balloon."

■ Draw a line from one picture to the matching picture.

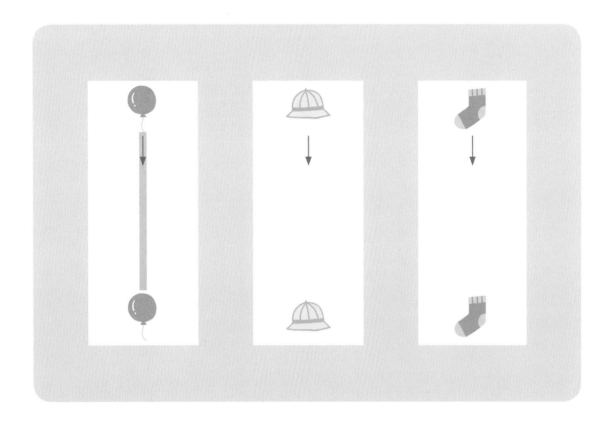

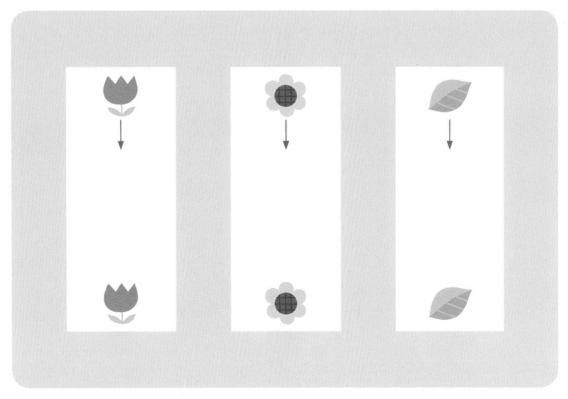

■Draw a line from one picture to the matching picture.

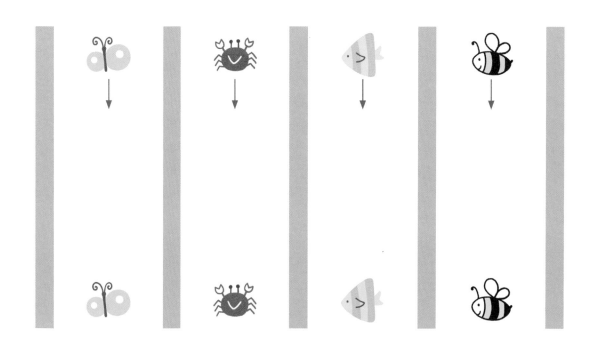

2 Drawing Straight Lines 2

Name

Date

To parents
At first, it is all right if your child's pencil pressure is light, if he or she does not draw perfectly straight lines, or draws outside of the area. Praise your child a lot, when he or she has completed the activity.

■ Draw a line from one picture to the matching picture.

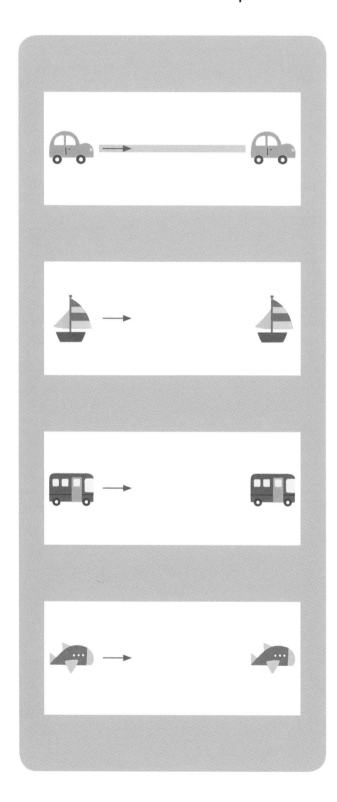

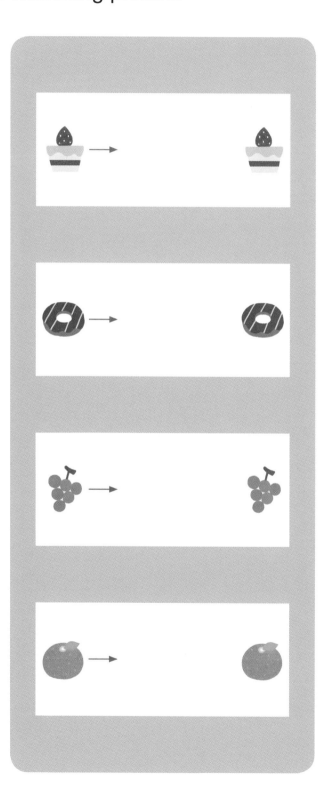

■Draw a line from one picture to the matching picture.

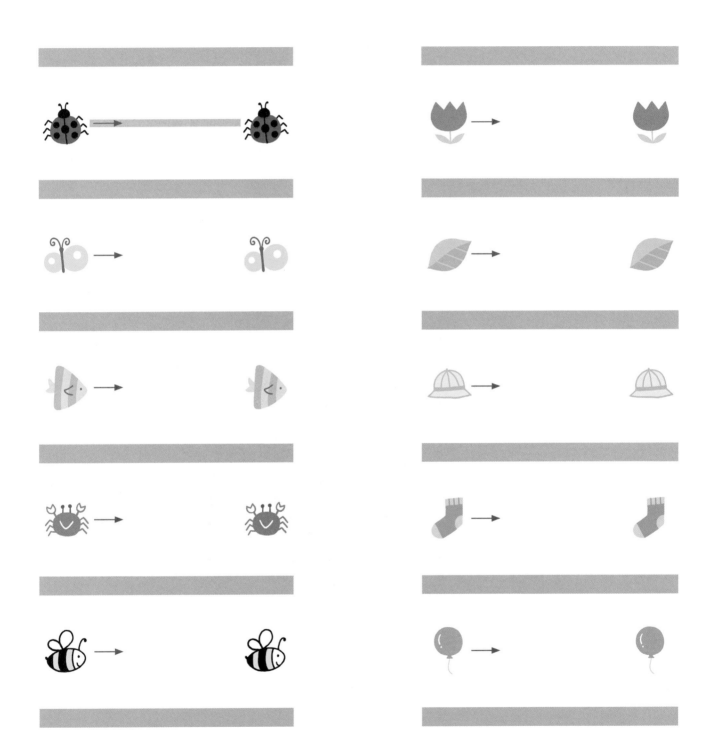

Drawing Straight Lines 3

Name

Date

To parents
This book helps your child develop pencil-stroke skills as he or she writes straight and curved lines in an area that starts wider and becomes narrower. The activities gradually become more difficult throughout the workbook. It is important that your child enjoys learning while completing the activities, even if he or she does not complete them perfectly.

▪Draw a line from one picture to the matching picture.

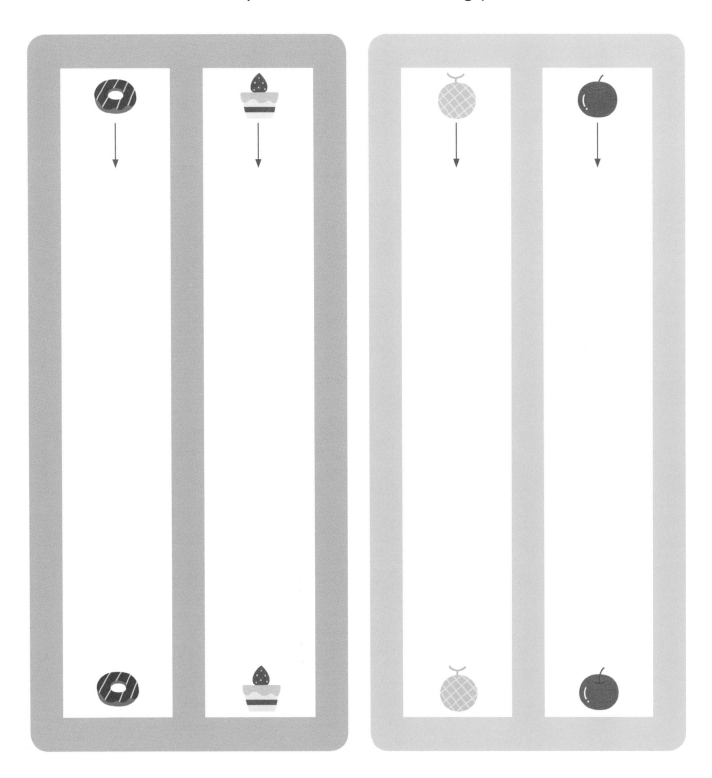

■Draw a line from one picture to the matching picture.

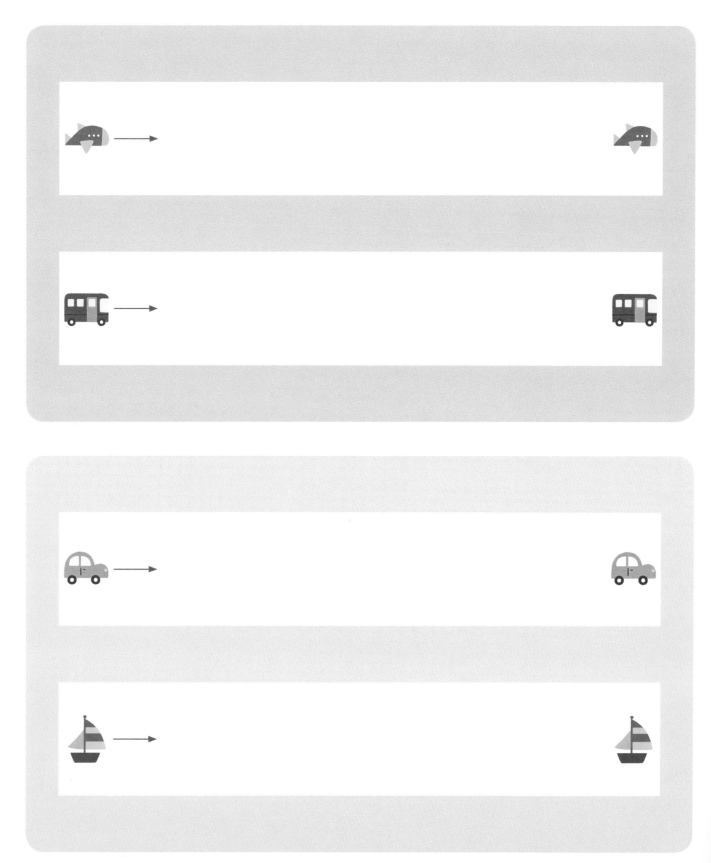

4 Drawing Diagonal Lines

Name

Date

To parents
This exercise teaches your child to draw diagonal lines. In the beginning, it is okay if your child draws outside of the area. If drawing the whole line in one stroke is too difficult, your child may pause in the middle.

■ Draw a line from one picture to the matching picture.

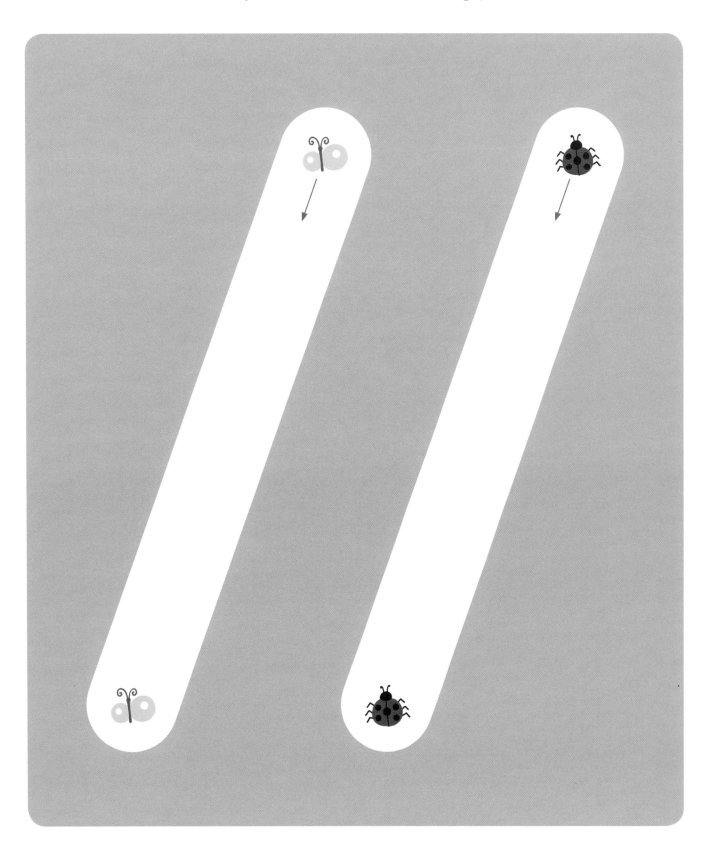

■Draw a line from one picture to the matching picture.

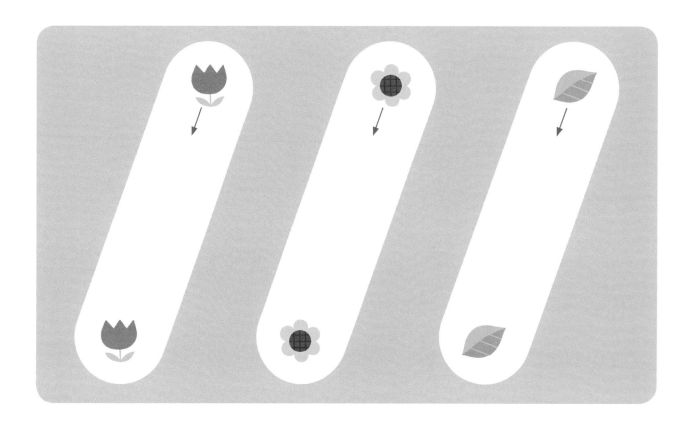

5 Drawing Jagged Lines

Name

Date

To parents
This exercise teaches your child to draw lines that change direction. Once your child learns to pause at the middle point, he or she may be able to do this exercise easier.

■Draw a line from one picture to the matching picture.

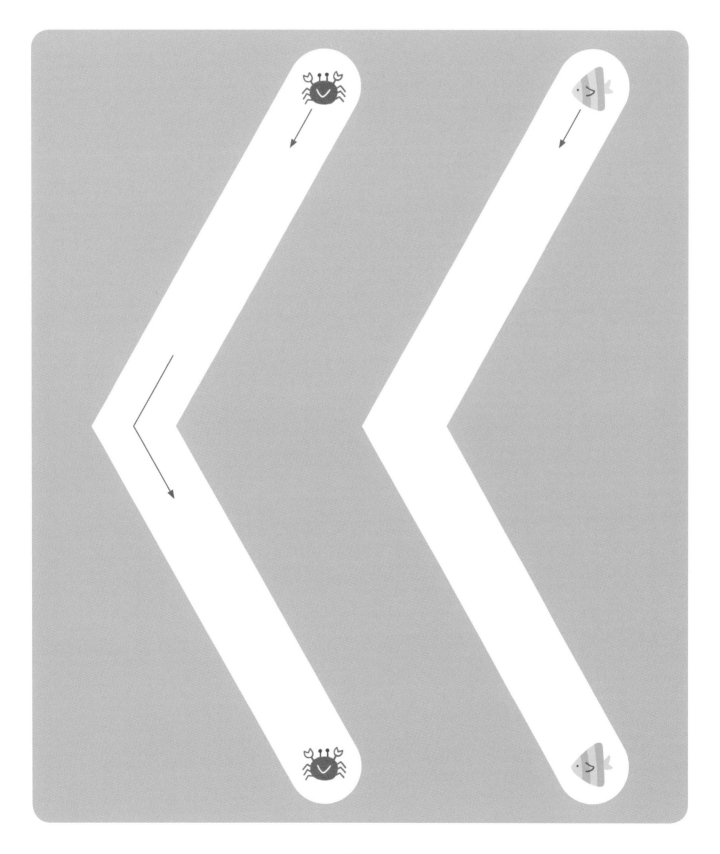

■Draw a line from one picture to the matching picture.

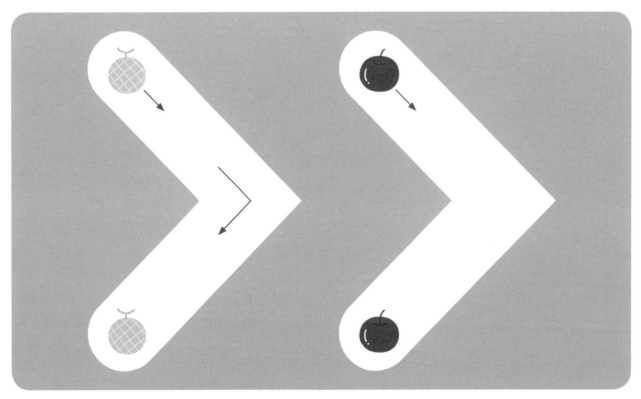

6 Drawing Curved Lines I

Name

Date

To parents
This exercise teaches your child to draw curved lines. Have your child move the pencil slowly along the curved path. Guide your child's hand and draw together if necessary.

▪Draw a line from one picture to the matching picture.

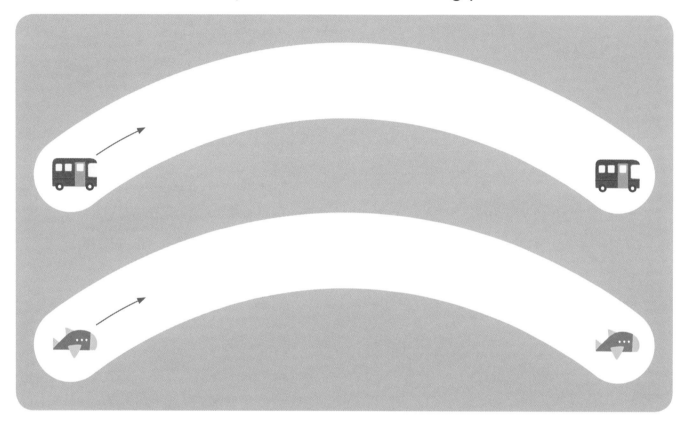

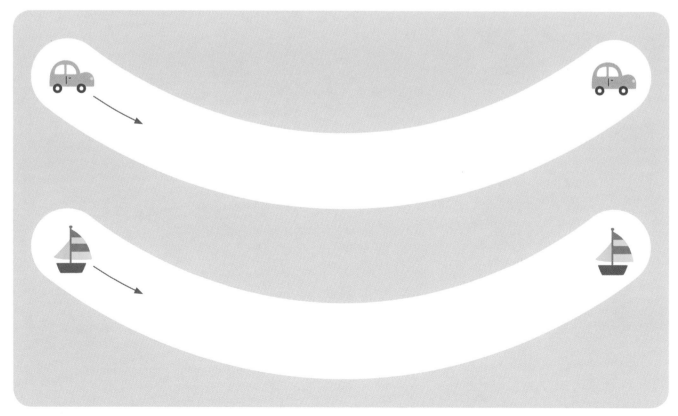

■Draw a line from one picture to the matching picture.

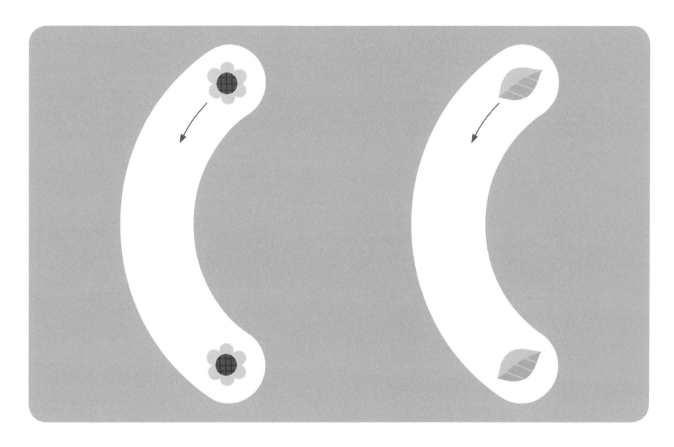

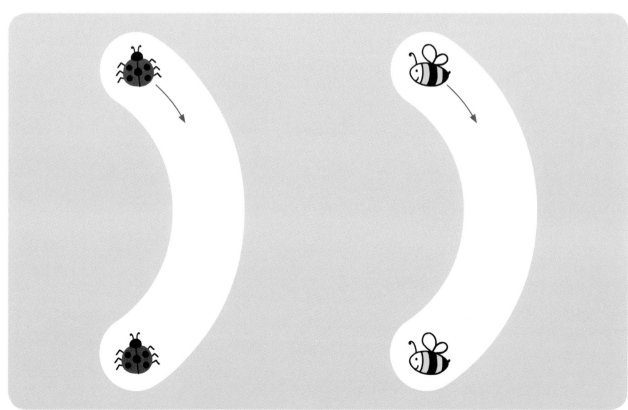

7 Drawing Circular Lines

Name

Date

To parents
This exercise teaches your child to draw circular lines. There may
be round shapes like a ball or a doughnut in your everyday life.
Drawing them with your child will greatly help his or her pencil-
stroke skills.

■Draw a line from one picture to the matching picture.

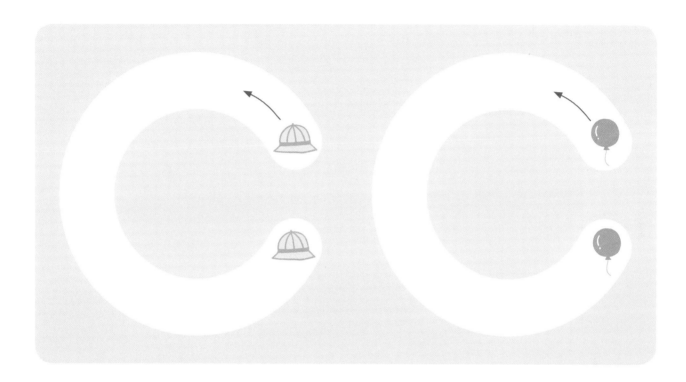

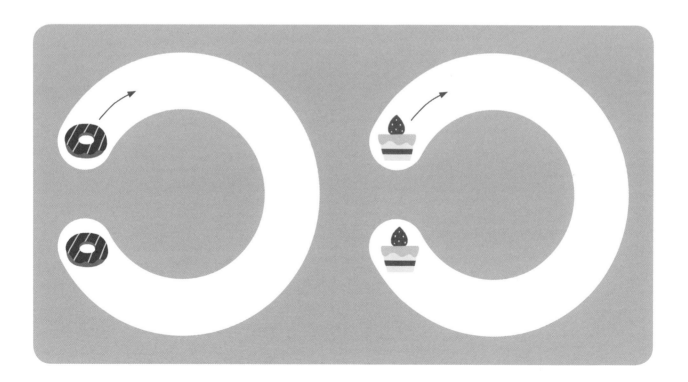

■Draw a line from one picture to the matching picture.

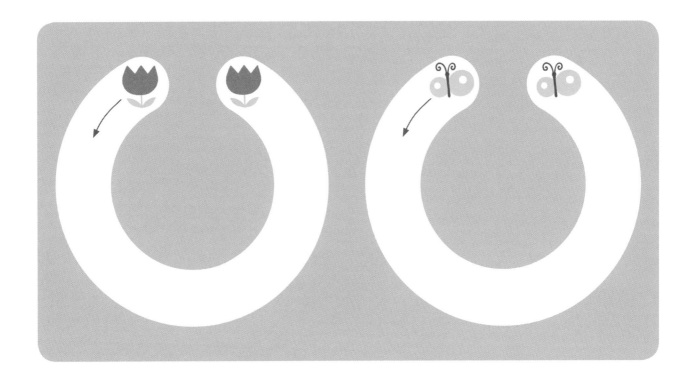

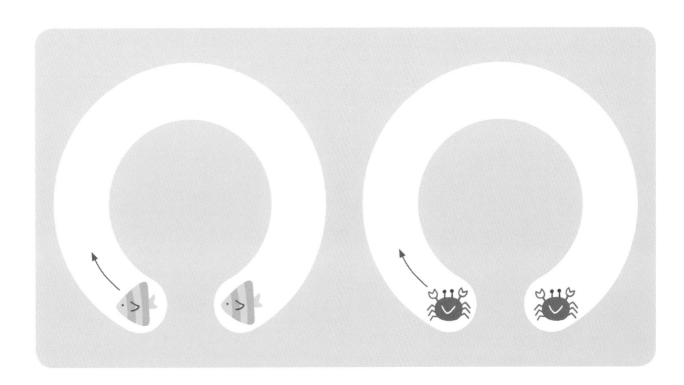

8 Drawing Lines That Cross

Name

Date

To parents
There is a crossing point on each exercise. Make sure your child follows the arrows at the crossing point so that he or she draws in the correct direction. It may be a good idea to have your child trace the path with his or her finger before drawing with a pencil.

■ Draw a line from one picture to the matching picture.

■Draw a line from one picture to the matching picture.

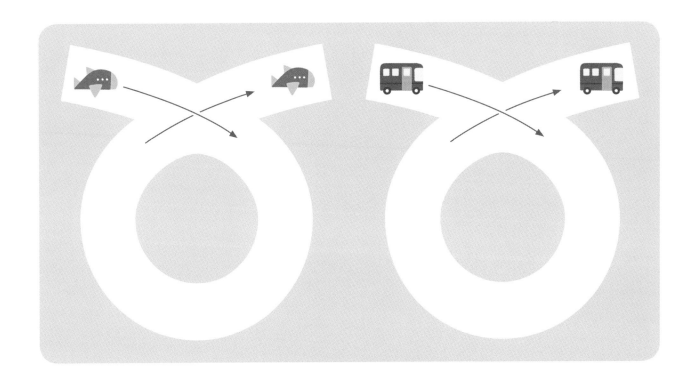

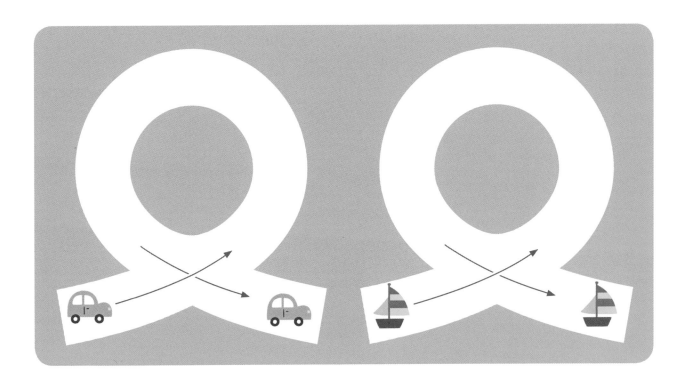

16

9 Drawing Zigzag Lines and Lines That Cross

Name

Date

To parents
From this page on, the paths are narrower. Encourage your child to avoid drawing outside of the area little by little. On this page, your child will learn to draw zigzag lines. If it is difficult for your child, allow him or her to pause at each corner.

■Draw a line from one picture to the matching picture.

17

■Draw a line from one picture to the matching picture.

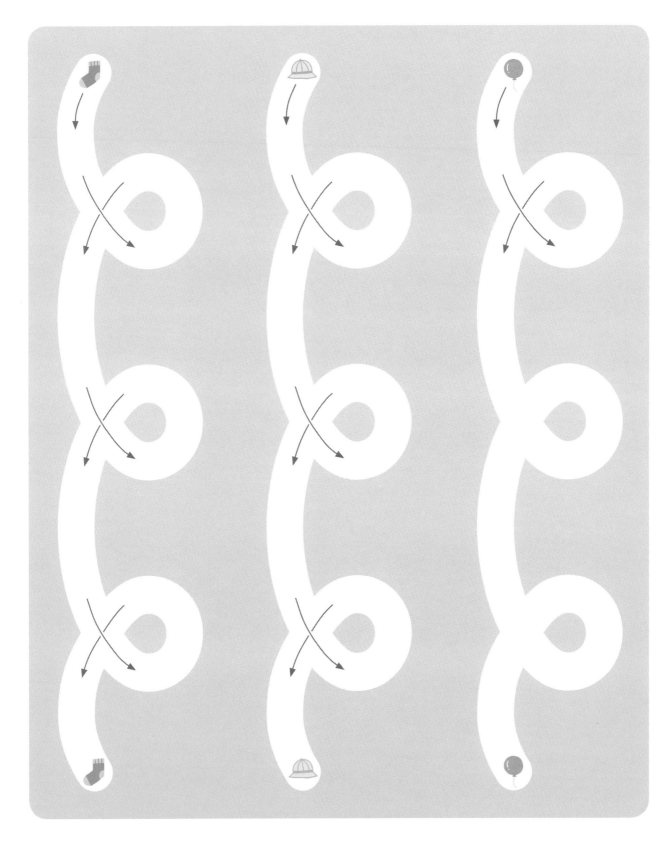

10 Drawing Curved Lines 2

Name

Date

To parents
The following exercises are to practice drawing longer lines. If drawing the whole line in one stroke is too difficult, your child may pause in the middle.

■Draw a line from one picture to the matching picture.

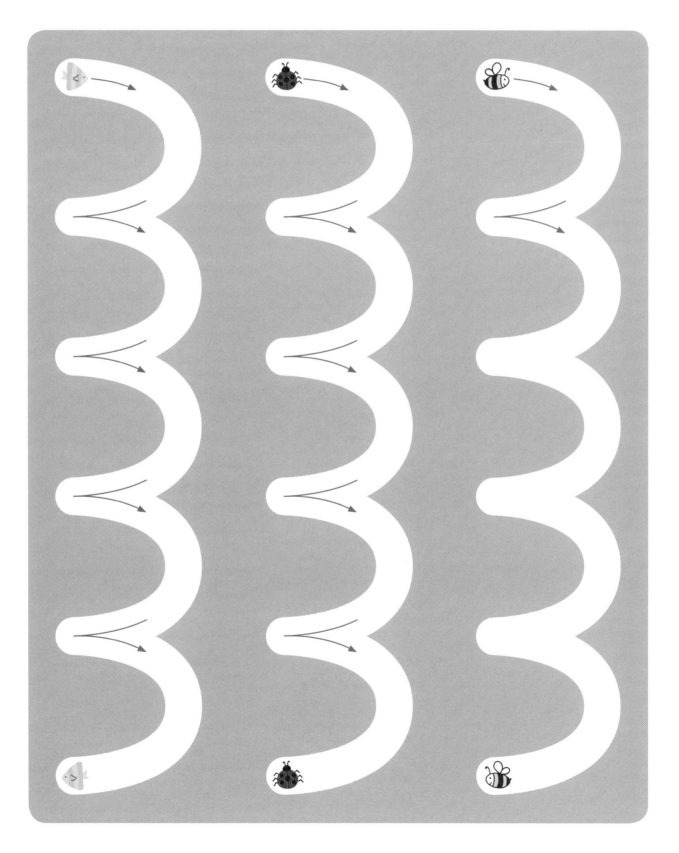

■Draw a line from one picture to the matching picture.

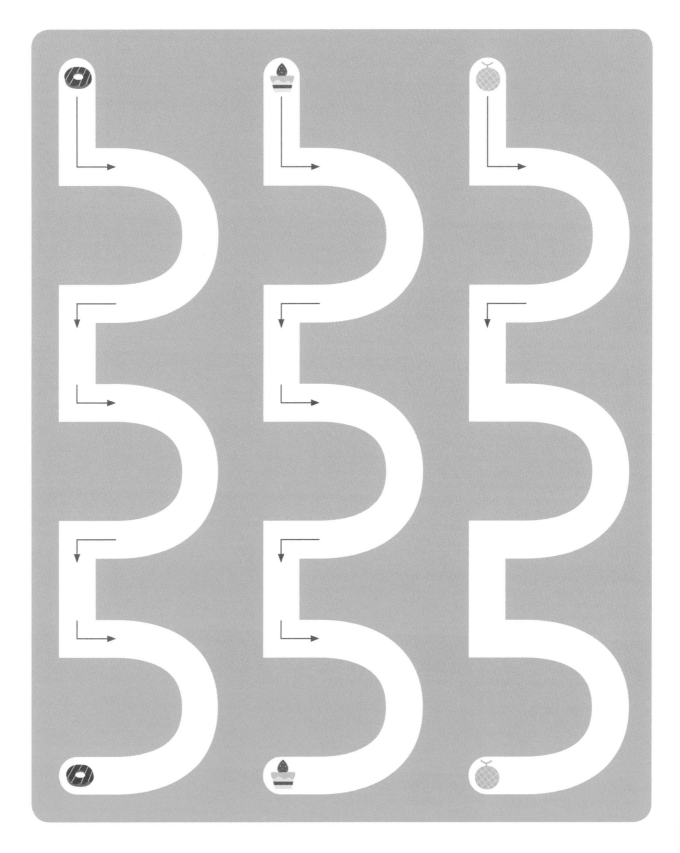

Drawing Curved Lines 3

Name

Date

To parents
Your child has practiced drawing various lines so far. All of the exercises will help your child learn how to write numbers properly. If your child cannot draw well, it is good to review the previous exercises and to draw lines repeatedly using crayons or colored pencils.

■Draw a line from one picture to the matching picture.

■Draw a line from one picture to the matching picture.

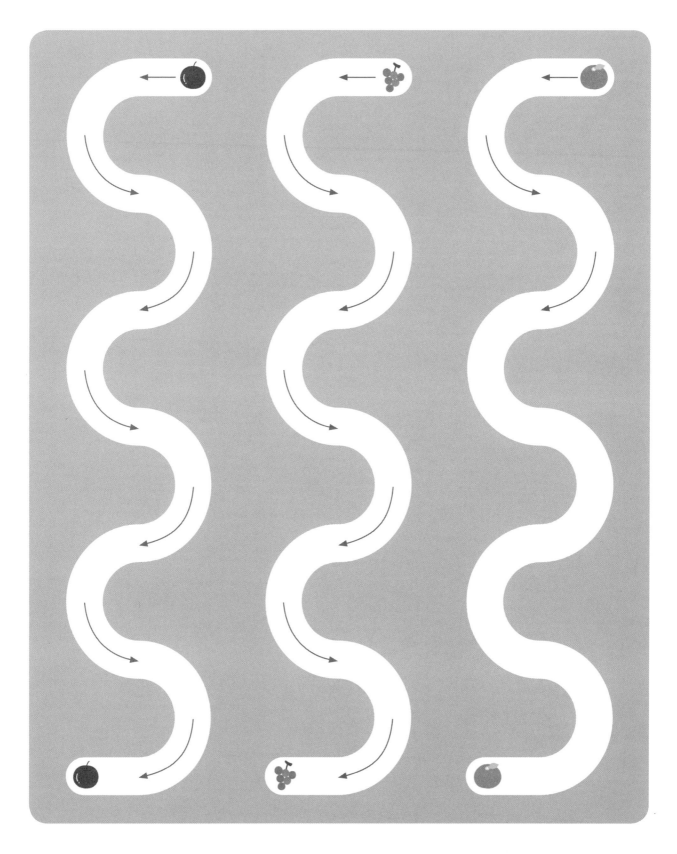

12 Number Puzzle 1 to 3
Apple

Name

Date

To parents
From this page on, your child will learn how to say the numbers as he or she improves the pencil-stroke skills. Have your child draw a line saying "one, two, three." In the beginning, it is all right if your child draws outside of the area. Praise your child a lot, when he or she has completed the activity.

Draw a line from 1 to 3 in order while saying each number.

Watermelon

■Draw a line from 1 to 3 in order while saying each number.

Name

Date

To parents
Guide your child's hand and draw together if necessary. It may be a good idea to have your child trace the path with his or her finger before drawing with a pencil.

■Draw a line from 1 to 4 in order while saying each number.

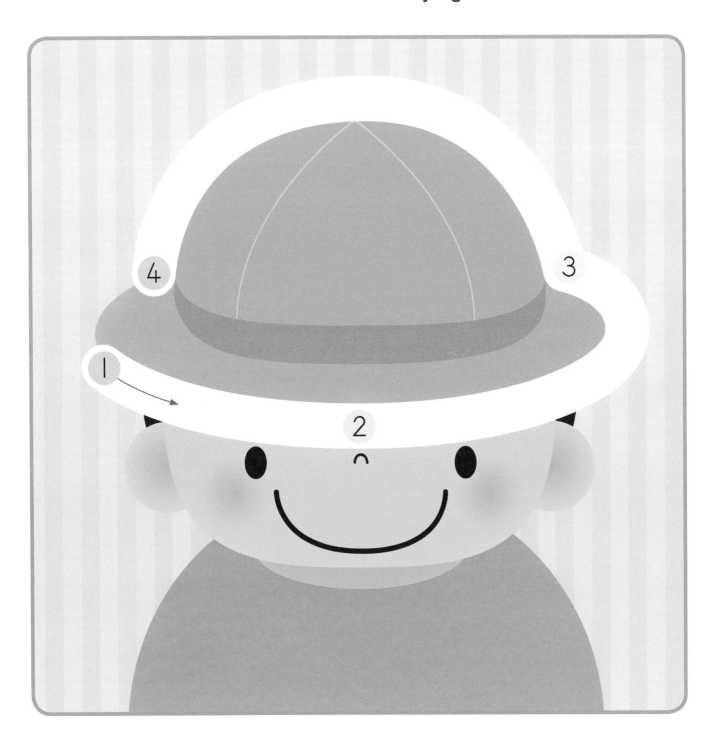

Colored Pencil

■Draw a line from 1 to 4 in order while saying each number.

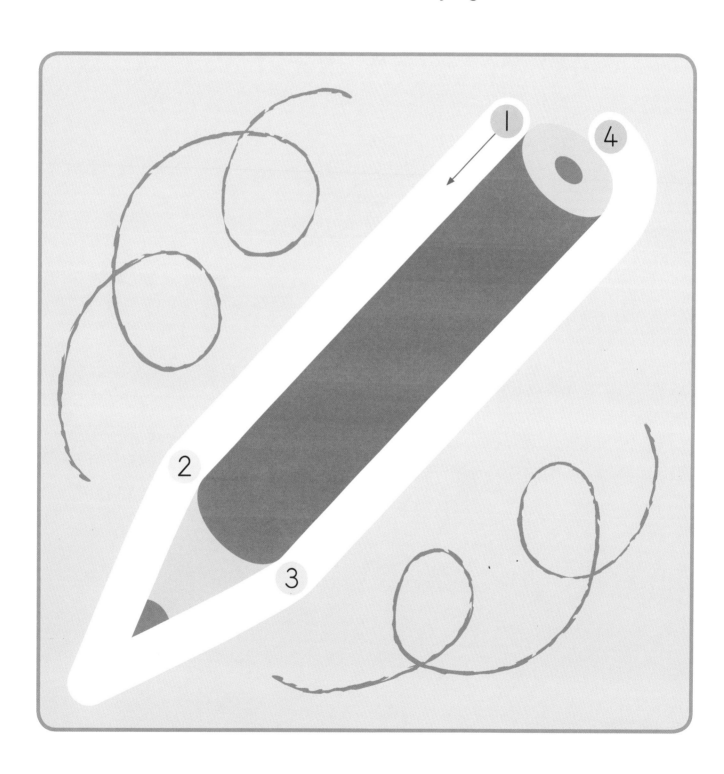

Name

Date

To parents
Your child will learn more numbers gradually. If your child cannot say some numbers well, teach him or her how to say them. After drawing a line, it may be good to say the numbers at the bottom of the page aloud. The numbers in the red circles are what your child has already learned in this book.

■Draw a line from I to 5 in order while saying each number.

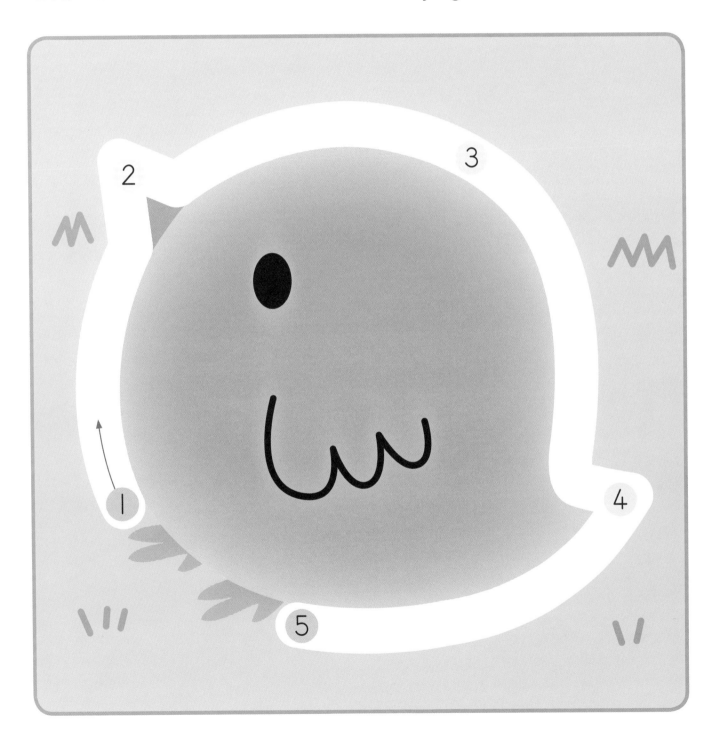

Ladybug

▪Draw a line from 1 to 5 in order while saying each number.

15 Number Puzzle 1 to 6
House

Name

Date

To parents
Guide your child's hand and draw together if necessary. It may be a good idea to have your child trace the path with his or her finger before drawing with a pencil.

■Draw a line from 1 to 6 in order while saying each number.

Car

■Draw a line from 1 to 6 in order while saying each number.

16 Number Puzzle 1 to 7
Juice

Name

Date

To parents
The activities will gradually have more curved lines. It is all right if your child draws outside of the area. The important thing is that your child draws slowly and carefully while saying the numbers.

■ Draw a line from 1 to 7 in order while saying each number.

Star

■Draw a line from 1 to 7 in order while saying each number.

17 | Number Puzzle 1 to 8 Eggplant

Name

Date

To parents
Praise your child's good work as much as possible, such as saying the numbers without mistakes, drawing a line within the area, and drawing a steady line.

■Draw a line from 1 to 8 in order while saying each number.

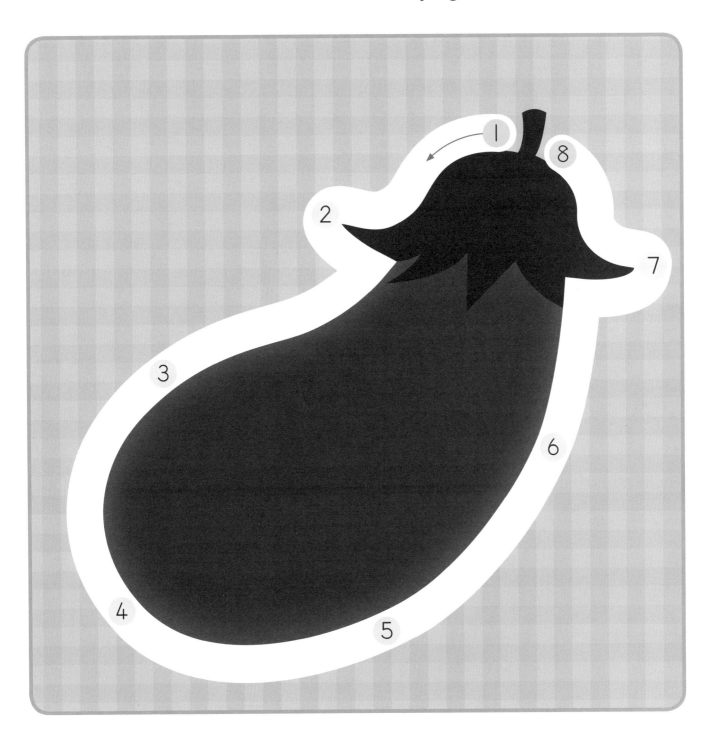

Dolphin

■Draw a line from 1 to 8 in order while saying each number.

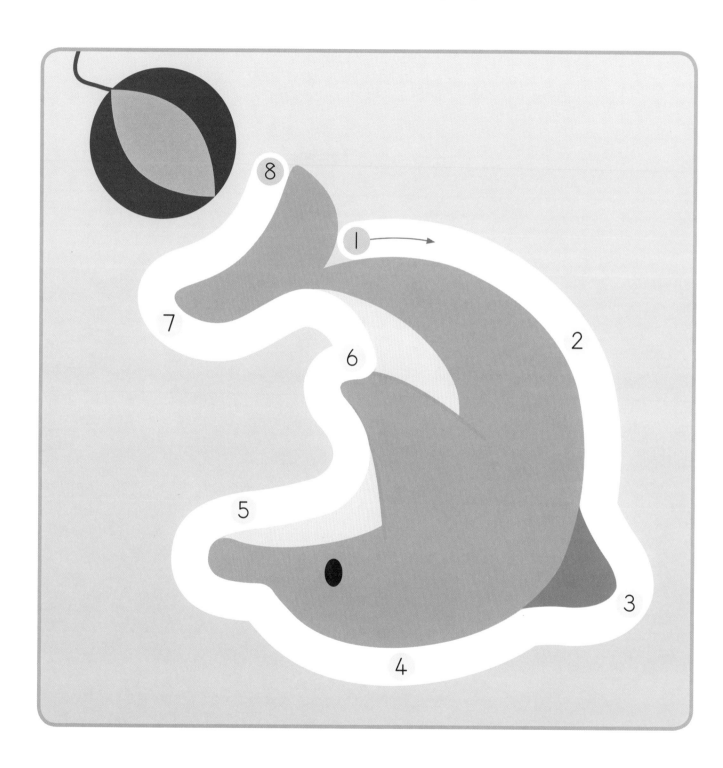

18 Number Puzzle 1 to 9 Umbrella

Name

Date

To parents
From this page on, the paths are narrower. It is all right if your child draws outside of the area. Praise your child a lot, when he or she has completed the activity.

■Draw a line from 1 to 9 in order while saying each number.

Scissors

■Draw a line from 1 to 9 in order while saying each number.

19 Number Puzzle 1 to 10 Tulip

Name

Date

To parents
Have your child draw a line and say the numbers "one, two, three…" aloud as he or she completes the activity. Now your child has learned 1 to 10. If your child cannot say some numbers well, have him or her practice more by saying them aloud together.

■ Draw a line from 1 to 10 in order while saying each number.

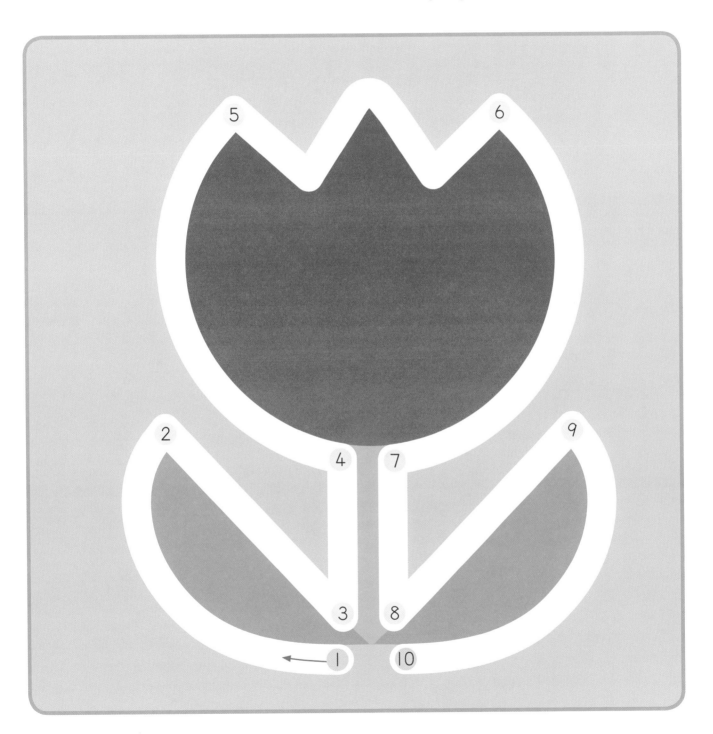

Sunfish

■Draw a line from 1 to 10 in order while saying each number.

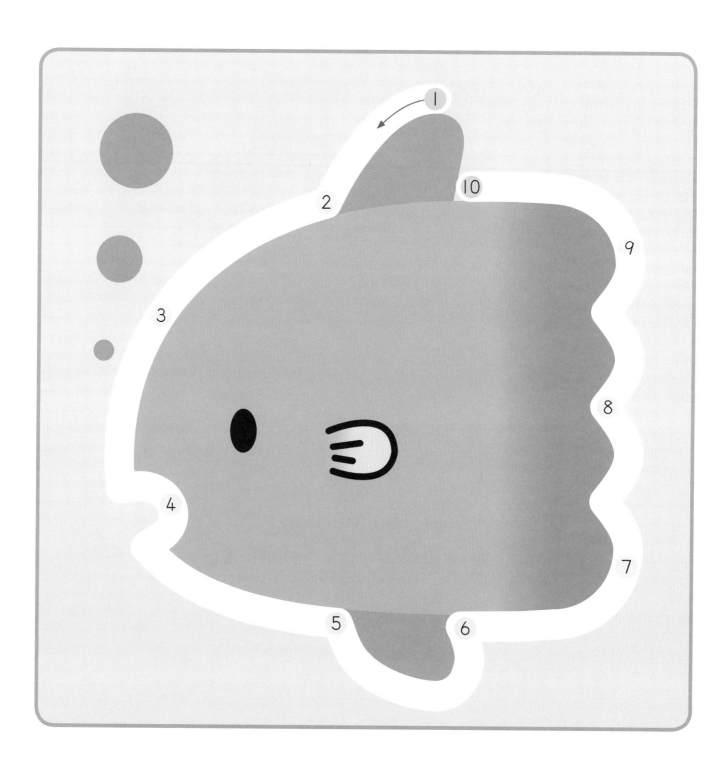

Name

Date

To parents
We hope that your child has found this book fun so far. If necessary, we recommend our "My Book of EASY MAZES" so that your child can improve the pencil-stroke skills: to draw steady lines and to draw lines within the designated area.

■ Draw a line from 1 to 10 in order while saying each number.

Sheep

▪ Draw a line from 1 to 10 in order while saying each number.

21 Writing Number 1

Name

Date

To parents
From this page on, there are exercises for writing 1 to 10. Tell your child that he or she should start with ● and draw to ★. The stroke path is fairly wide, but it is all right if your child draws outside of the area at first.

▪ Write the number 1 and say it aloud.

one

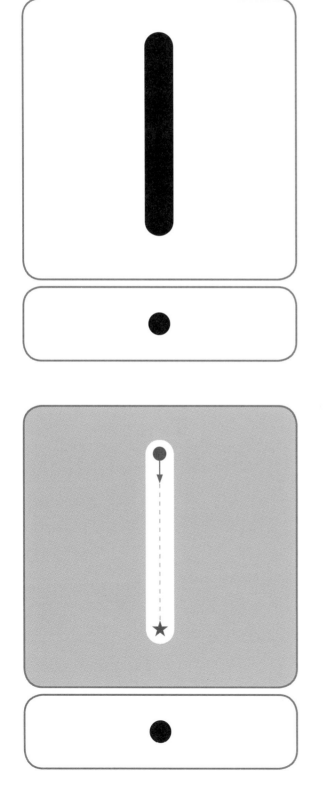

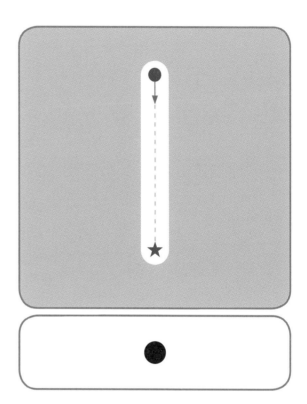

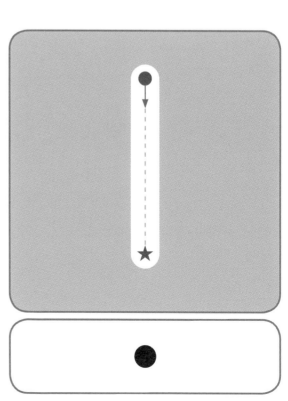

■Write the number 1 and say it aloud.

one

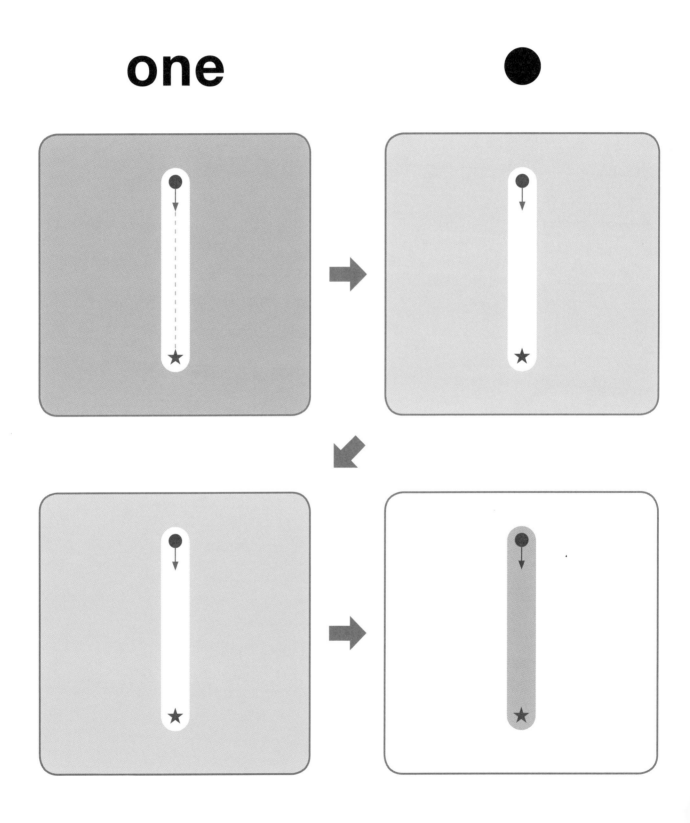

Writing Number 2

Name

Date

To parents
If your child does not know what to do in this activity, advise him or her to draw a line from ● to ★. Praise your child a lot, when he or she has completed the activity.

■ Write the number 2 and say it aloud.

two

■Write the number 2 and say it aloud.

two

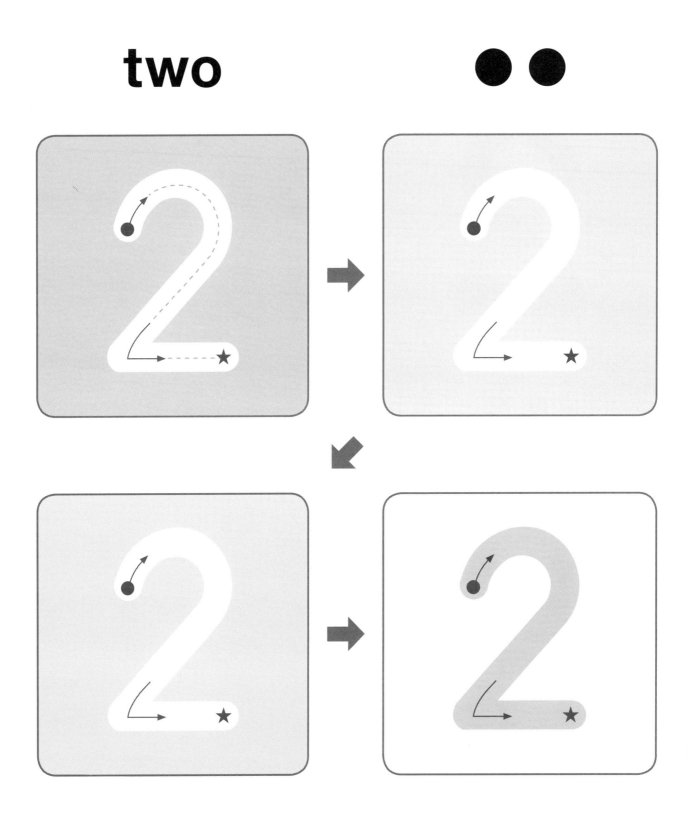

23 Writing Number 3

Name

Date

To parents
If it is challenging for your child to write the number 3, guide your child's hand and write it together. It may be a good idea to have your child trace the number with his or her finger before writing with a pencil.

■ Write the number 3 and say it aloud.

three

■Write the number 3 and say it aloud.

three

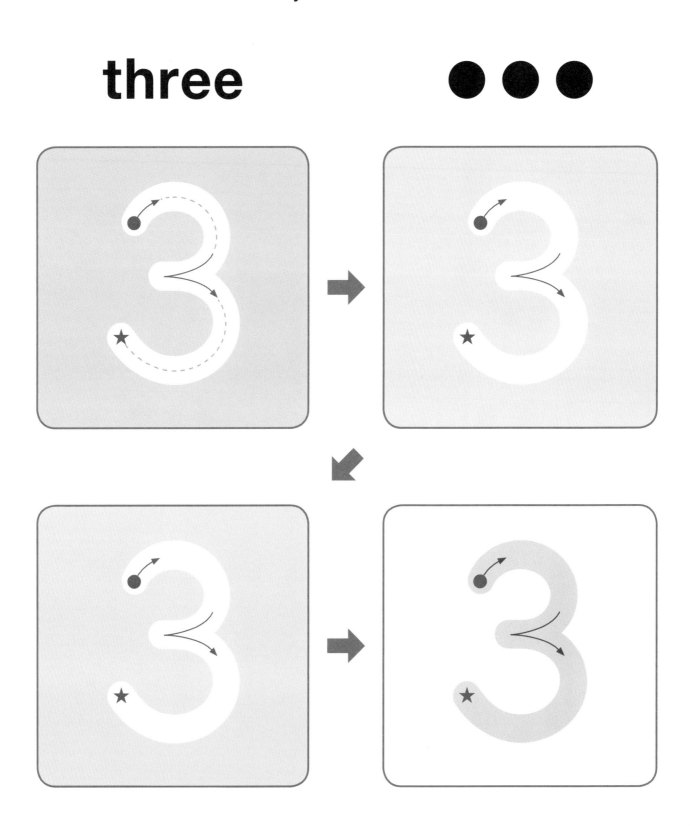

24 Writing Number 4

Name

Date

To parents
Have your child be careful to write the number 4 in the right stroke order. Tell him or her that the number 4 is written in two strokes and to start at ❶.

■Write the number 4 and say it aloud.

four

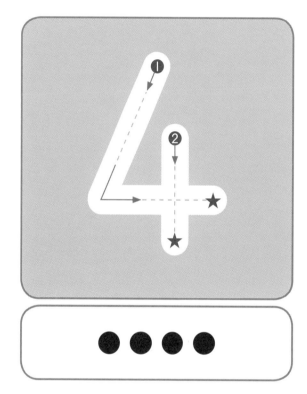

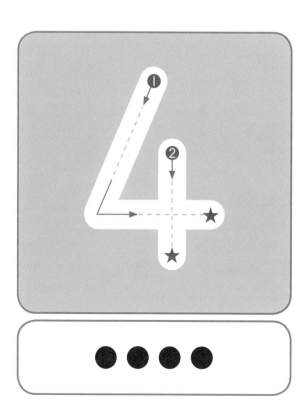

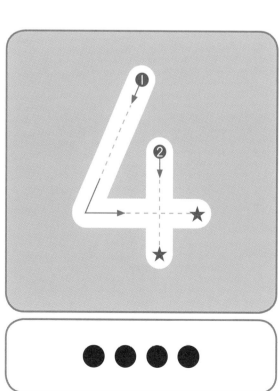

■Write the number 4 and say it aloud.

four

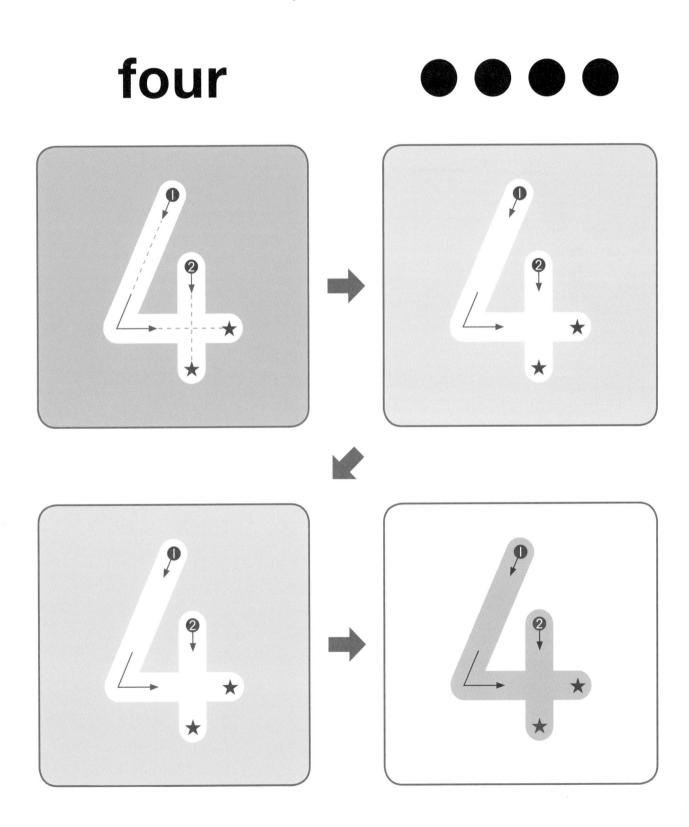

25 Writing Number 5

Name

Date

To parents
Have your child carefully write the number 5 in the right stroke order. It may be good to have him or her count the number of dots (●) one by one while pointing to them or to trace the path with his or her finger before writing with a pencil.

■ Write the number 5 and say it aloud.

five

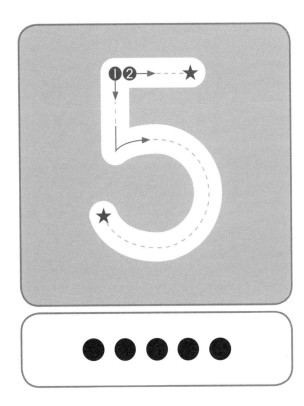

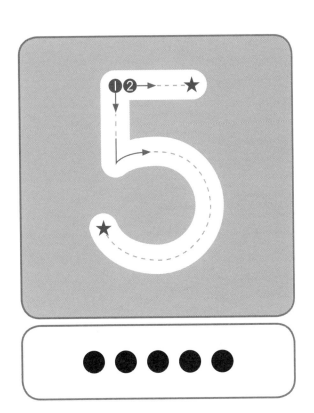

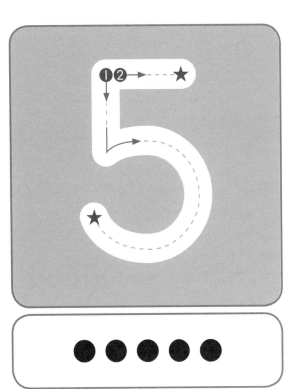

■Write the number 5 and say it aloud.

five

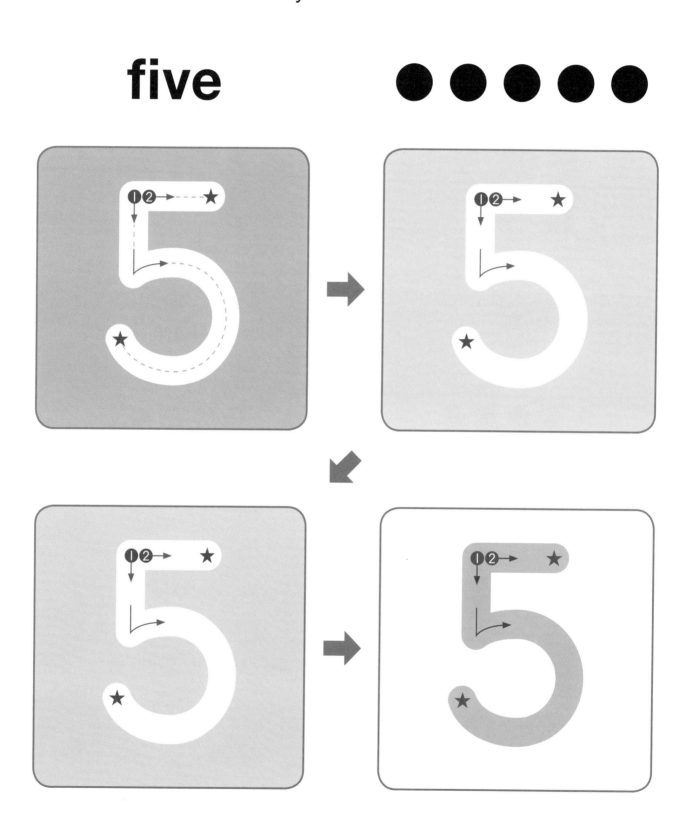

Writing Numbers 1 to 5

Name

Date

To parents
The paths are narrower than the previous pages. In the beginning, it is all right if your child draws outside of the area.

■Write the numbers and say them aloud.

 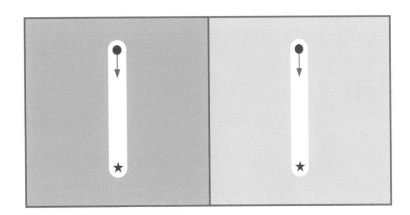

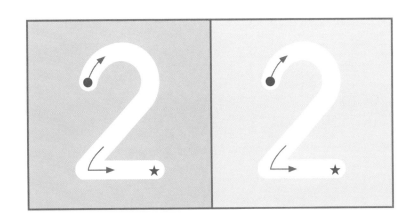

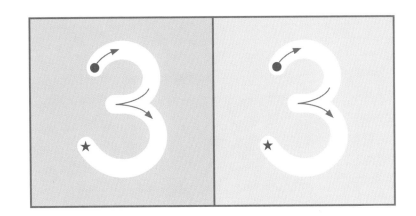

■Write the numbers and say them aloud.

4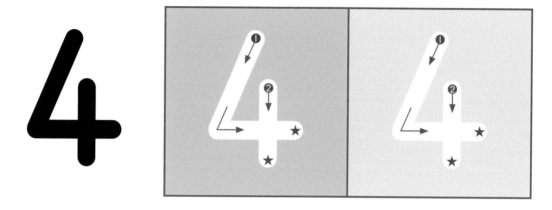

5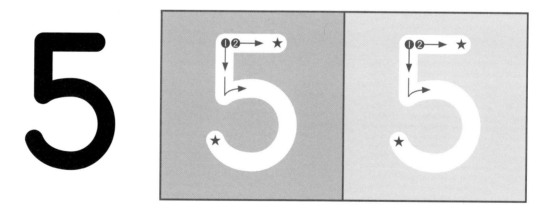

Writing Numbers
1 to 5

Name

Date

To parents
On the backside of this page, the exercise is to have your child write the numbers without arrows and paths as guides. It may be challenging for your child to do many exercises on one page. Praise your child a lot, when he or she has completed the activity.

■Write the numbers and say them aloud.

■Write the numbers and say them aloud.

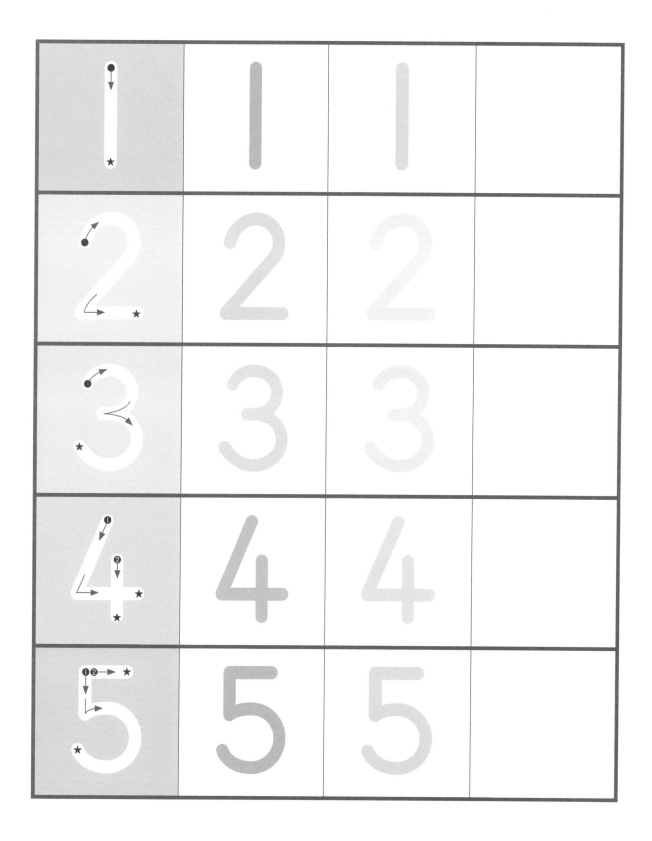

28 Writing Numbers 1 to 5

Name

Date

To parents
Make sure that your child writes the numbers 1 to 5 well. It is all right if their pencil pressure is light or they do not draw perfectly straight lines. Encourage them to practice writing the numbers repeatedly.

■ Write the numbers and say them aloud.

■Write the numbers and say them aloud.

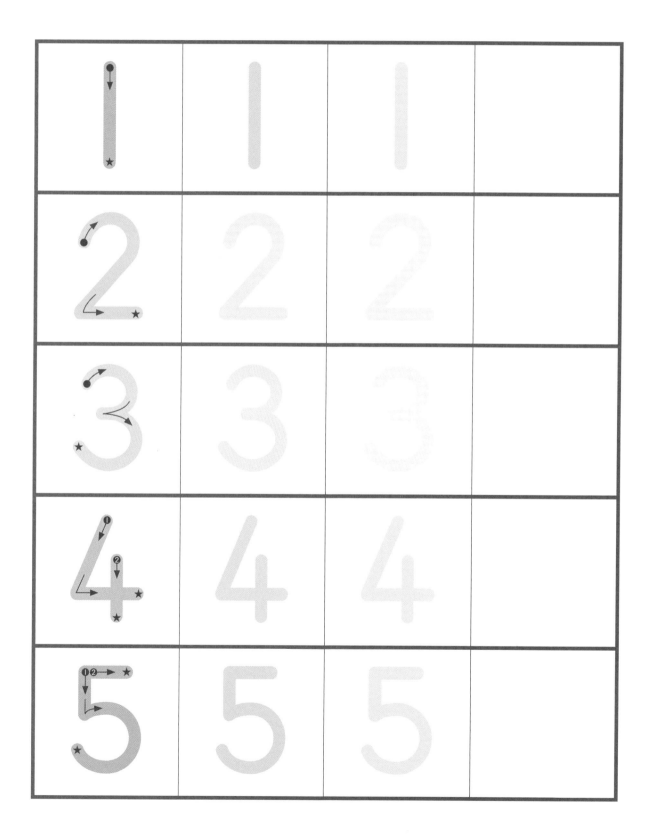

29 Writing Number 6

Name

Date

To parents
Have your child write the number as they say it aloud. The stroke
path is fairly wide, but it is all right if your child draws outside of
the area a little, as long as he or she draws steady lines.

■Write the number 6 and say it aloud.

six

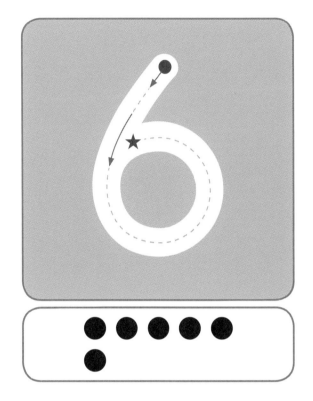

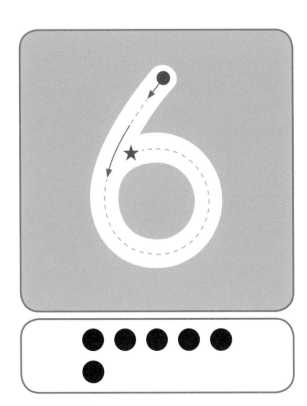

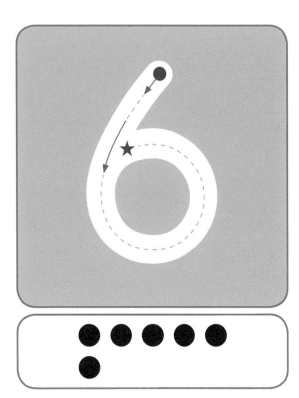

■Write the number 6 and say it aloud.

six

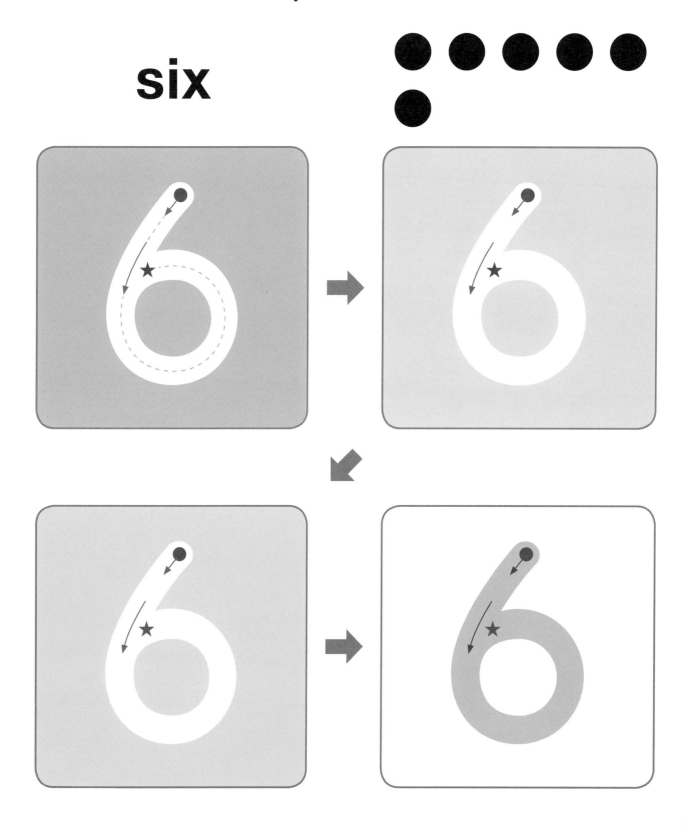

Name

Date

To parents
If necessary, advise your child to draw a line from ● to ★. It may be good to have him or her count the number of dots (●) one by one while pointing to them or to trace the path with his or her finger before writing with a pencil.

■ Write the number 7 and say it aloud.

seven

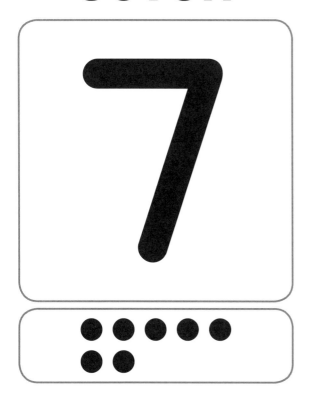

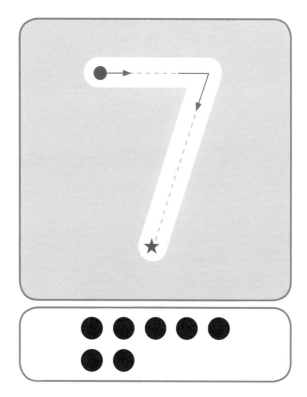

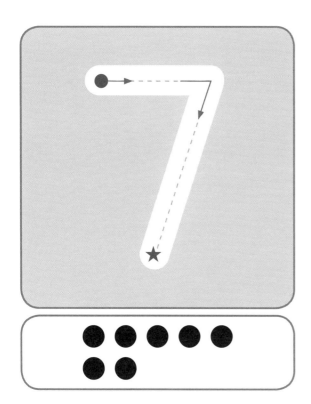

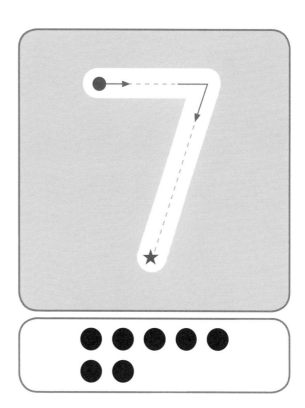

■Write the number 7 and say it aloud.

seven

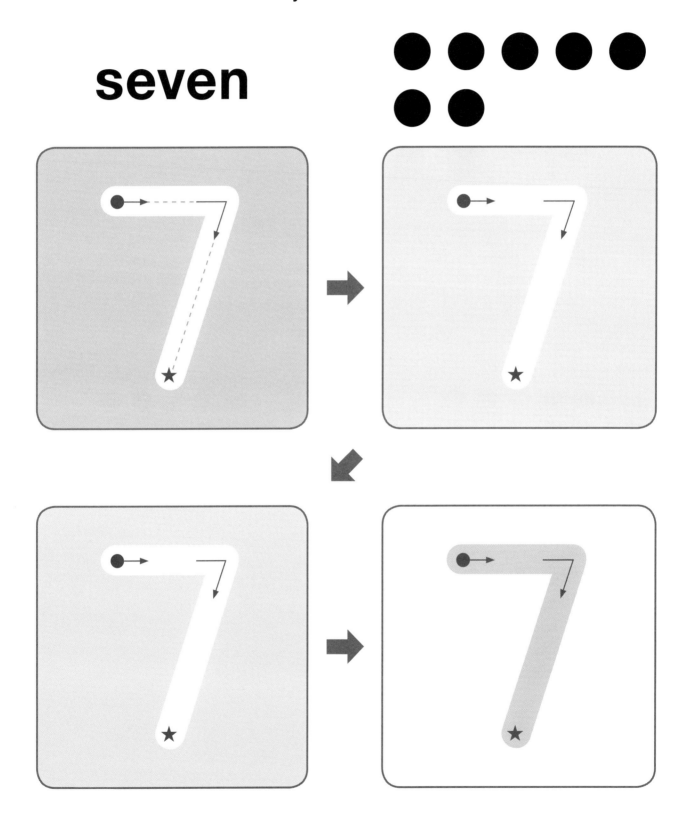

Name

Date

To parents
It is more difficult to write the number 8 than to write other numbers. In the beginning, it is all right if your child cannot write it well. Encourage him or her to practice writing it repeatedly.

■Write the number 8 and say it aloud.

eight

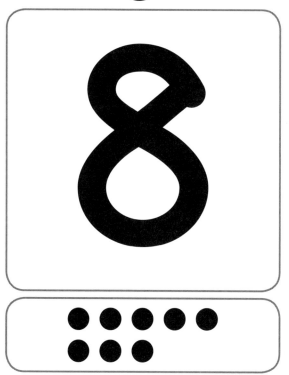

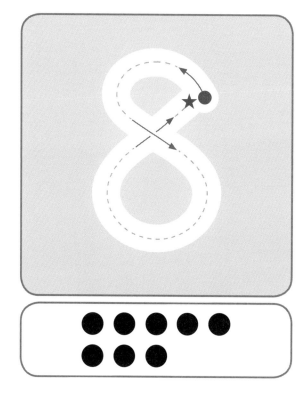

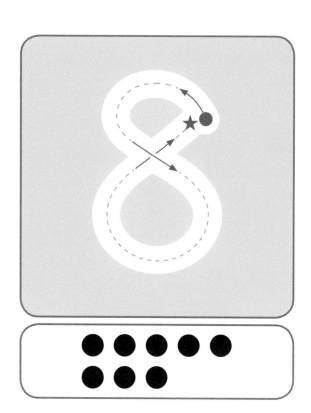

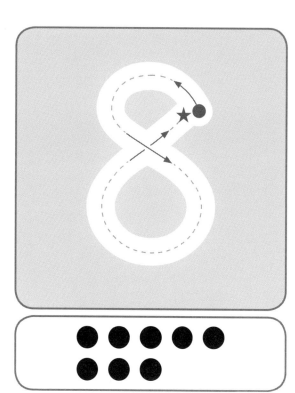

■Write the number 8 and say it aloud.

eight

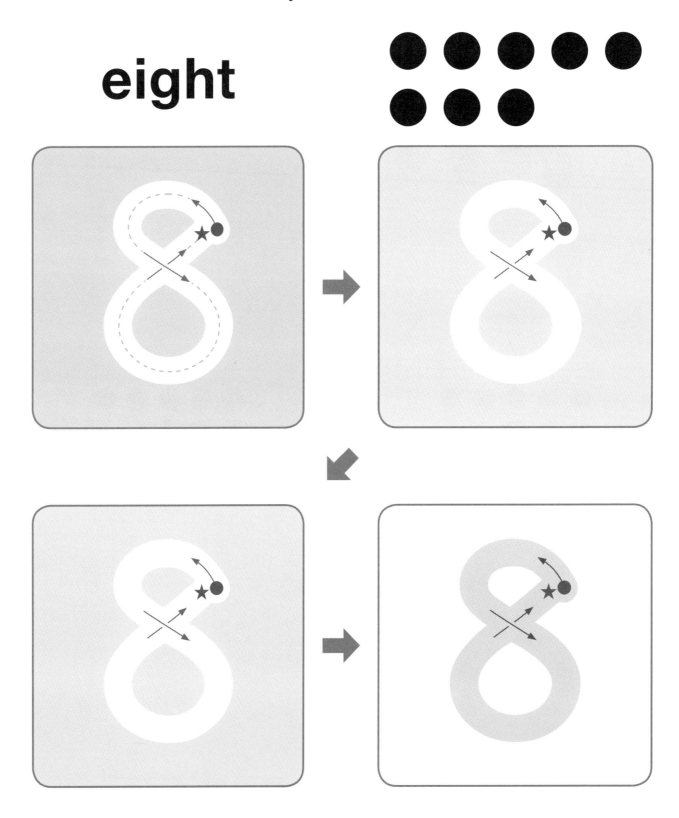

32 Writing Number 9

Name

Date

To parents
If it is challenging for your child to write the number 9, guide your child's hand and write together. Praise him or her a lot, when he or she has completed the activity.

■Write the number 9 and say it aloud.

nine

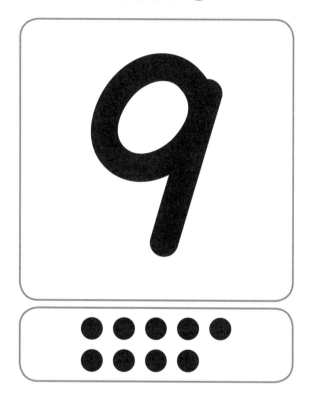

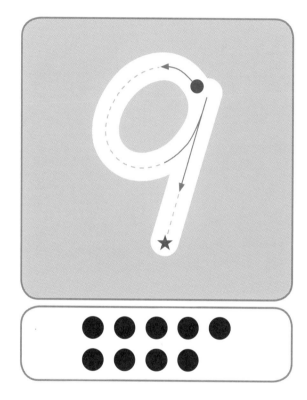

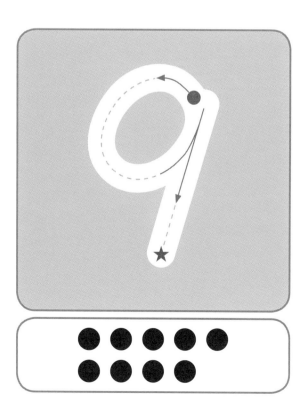

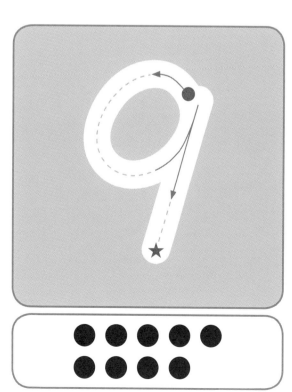

■Write the number 9 and say it aloud.

nine

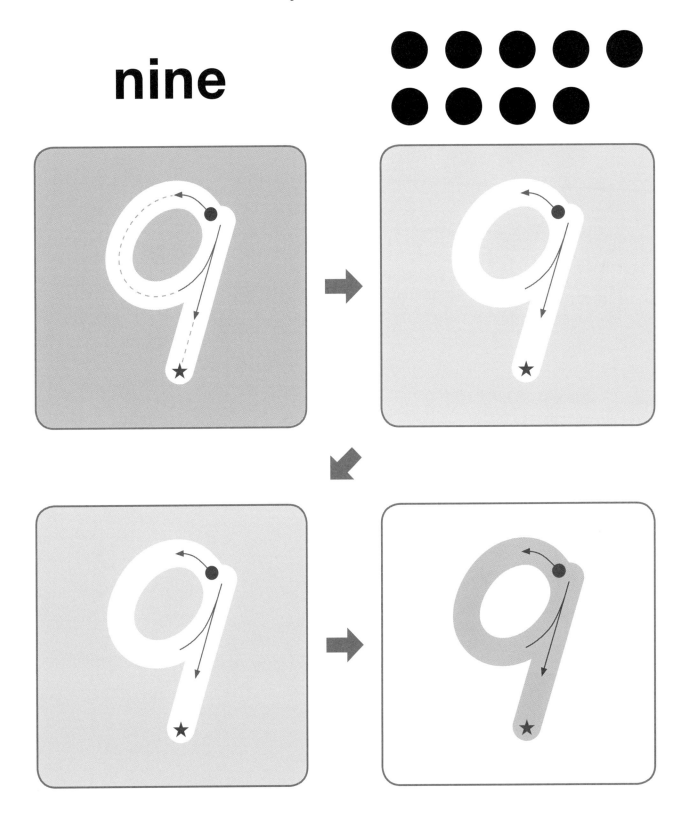

33 **Writing Number 10**

Name

Date

To parents
It may be good to have your child count the number of dots (●) one by one while pointing to them or to trace the path with his or her finger before writing with a pencil.

■Write the number 10 and say it aloud.

ten

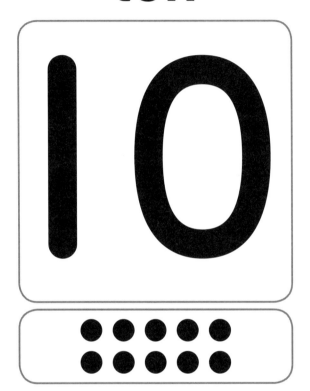

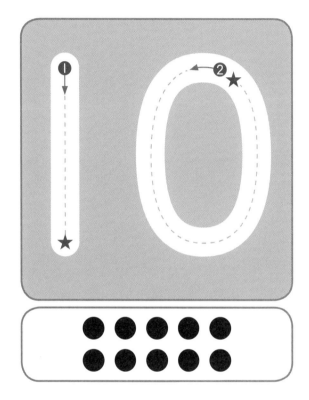

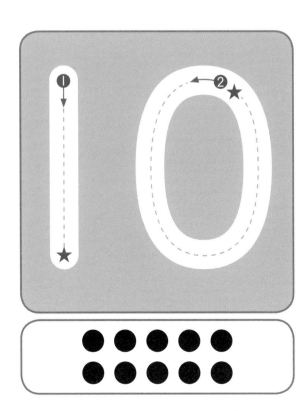

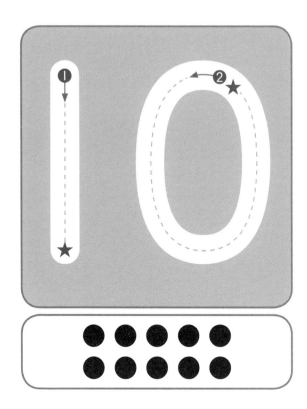

■Write the number 10 and say it aloud.

ten

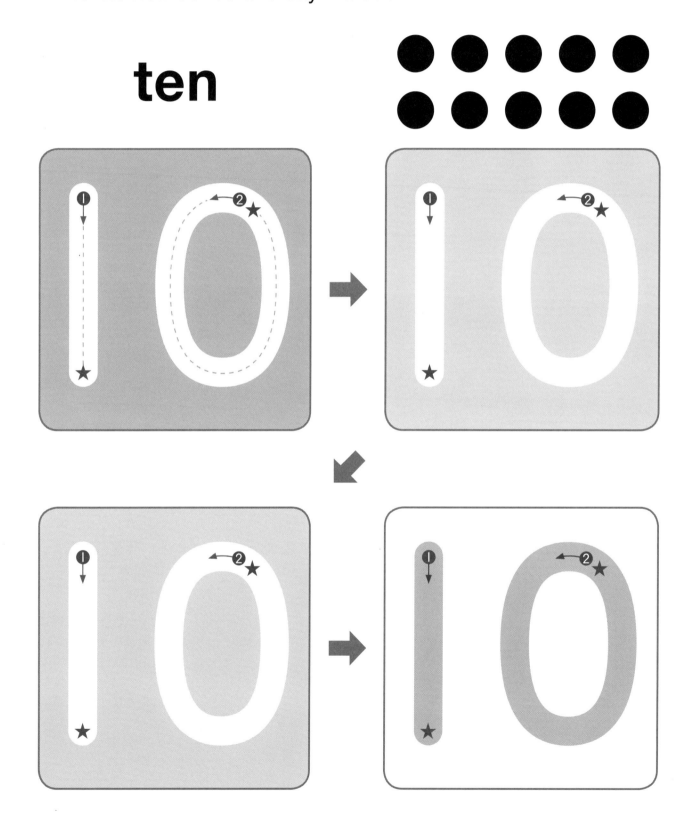

34 Writing Numbers 6 to 10

Name

Date

To parents
The paths are narrower than the previous pages. In the beginning, it is all right if your child draws outside of the area. Have him or her say the numbers aloud when writing them.

■ Write the numbers and say them aloud.

 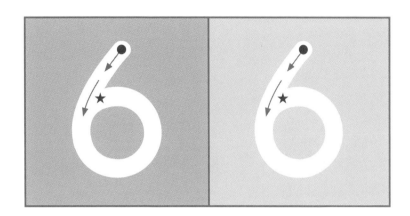

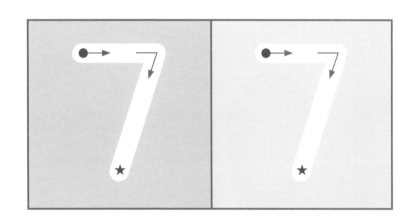

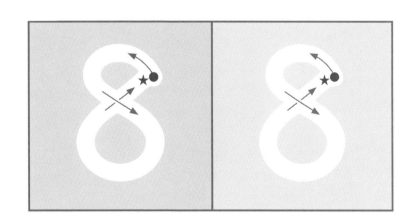

■Write the numbers and say them aloud.

9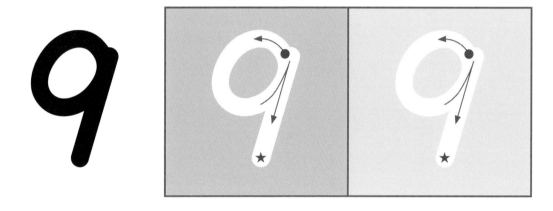

10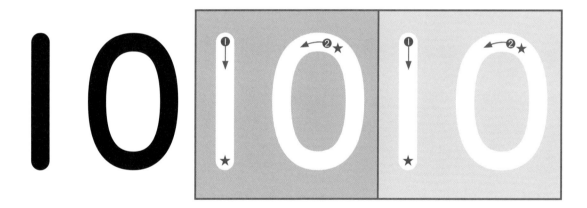

Writing Numbers
6 to 10

Name

Date

To parents
On the backside of this page, the exercise is to have your child write the numbers without arrows and paths as guides. It may be challenging for your child to do many exercises on one page. Praise him or her a lot, when he or she has completed the activity.

■Write the numbers and say them aloud.

•••• • 6	6	6
••••• •• 7	7	7
••••• ••• 8	8	8
••••• •••• 9	9	9
••••• ••••• 10	10	10

■Write the numbers and say them aloud.

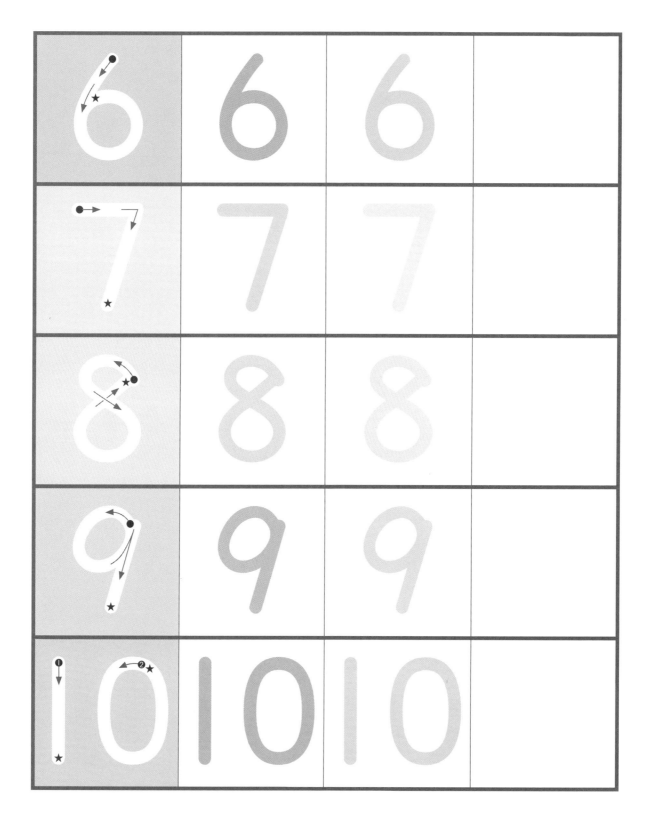

Writing Numbers
6 to 10

36

Name

Date

Make sure that your child writes the numbers 6 to 10 well. It is all right if their pencil pressure is light or they do not draw perfectly straight lines. Encourage them to practice writing the numbers repeatedly.

■Write the numbers and say them aloud.

71

■Write the numbers and say them aloud.

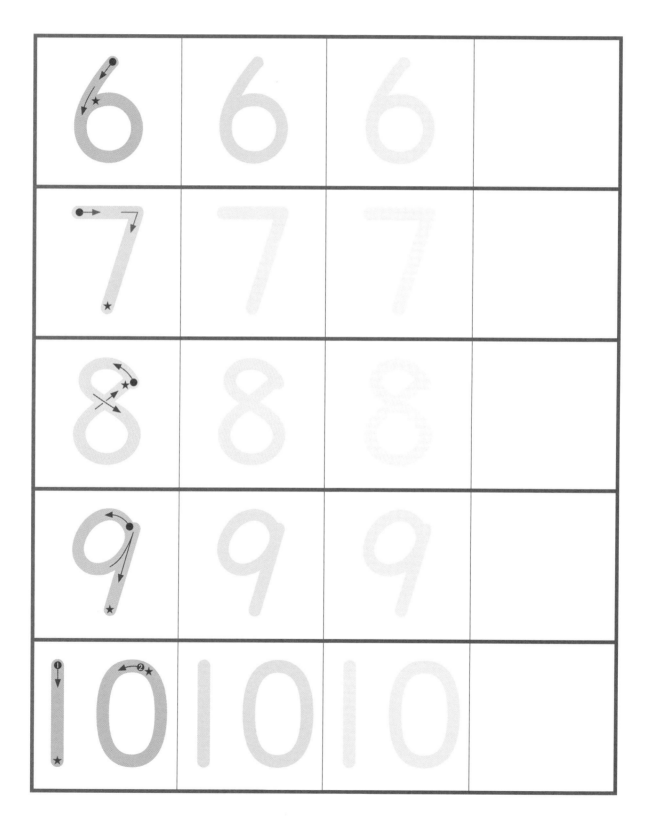

Name

Date

To parents
The following pages review the numbers 1 to 10. Have your child say the numbers aloud as he or she writes them. Praise your child's good work as much as possible, such as saying the numbers without mistakes or concentrating well while doing the exercise.

■ Write the numbers and say them aloud.

•	1	1
••	2	2
•••	3	3
••••	4	4
•••••	5	5

■Write the numbers and say them aloud.

●	● ●	● ● ●	● ● ● ●	● ● ● ● ●
1	2	3	4	5

●	● ●	● ● ●	● ● ● ●	● ● ● ● ●
1	2	3	4	5

●	● ●	● ● ●	● ● ● ●	● ● ● ● ●
1	2	3	4	5

Name

Date

To parents
We hope that your child has enjoyed this book so far. You might realize that your child has progressed in their pencil-stroke skills, compared to when they first started. Praise your child a lot for his or her hard work and improvement.

Write the numbers and say them aloud.

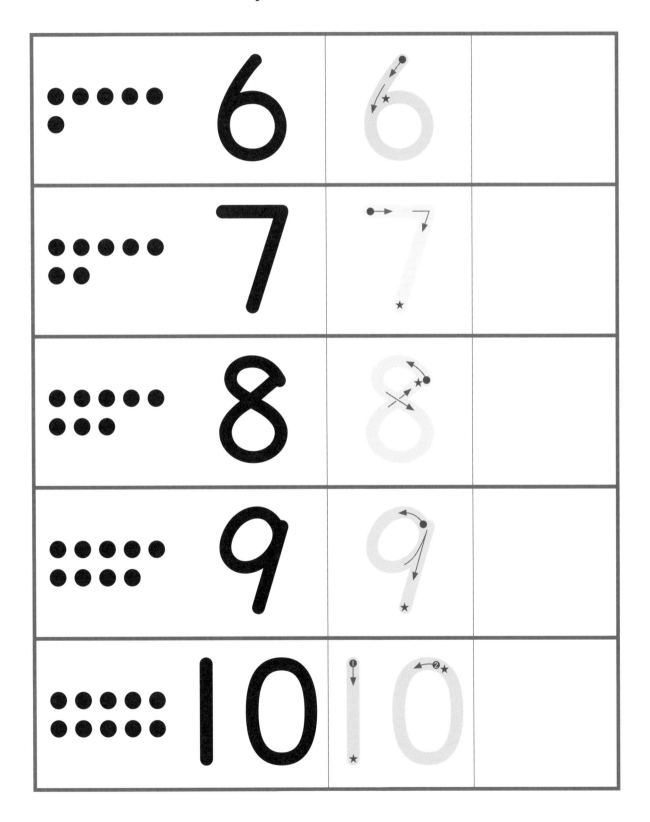

■Write the numbers and say them aloud.

● ● ● ● ● ●	● ● ● ● ● ● ●	● ● ● ● ● ● ● ●	● ● ● ● ● ● ● ● ●	● ● ● ● ● ● ● ● ● ●
6	7	8	9	10

● ● ● ● ● ●	● ● ● ● ● ● ●	● ● ● ● ● ● ● ●	● ● ● ● ● ● ● ● ●	● ● ● ● ● ● ● ● ● ●
6	7	8	9	10

● ● ● ● ● ●	● ● ● ● ● ● ●	● ● ● ● ● ● ● ●	● ● ● ● ● ● ● ● ●	● ● ● ● ● ● ● ● ● ●
6	7	8	9	10

Name

Date

To parents
When your child has finished this book, give him or her the Certificate of Achievement on which you can write his or her name and the date. Now that your child can read and write the numbers 1 to 10, we recommend our "My Book of NUMBERS 1 – 30" for further work.

▪Write the numbers and say them aloud.

1	2	3	4	5
6	7	8	9	10

1	2	3	4	5
6	7	8	9	10

■Write the numbers and say them aloud.

1	2	3	4	5
6	7	8	9	10

1				
				10

Certificate of Achievement

_____

is hereby congratulated on completing

My Book of Numbers 1-10

Presented on _____ , 20 _____

_____
Parent or Guardian